First edition for the United States and Canada published
in 2008 by Barron's Educational Series, Inc.

First edition of *Why Am I So Tired?*
first published for Great Britain in 2008 by Wayland,
a division of Hachette Children's Books

Text copyright © Pat Thomas 2008
Illustrations copyright © Lesley Harker 2008

All inquiries should be addressed to:
Barron's Educational Series, Inc.
250 Wireless Boulevard
Hauppauge, New York 11788
www.barronseduc.com

Library of Congress Control Number: 2007943053

ISBN-13: 978-0-7641-3899-7
ISBN-10: 0-7641-3899-5

Printed in China
9 8 7 6 5 4 3 2 1

Disclaimer

Why Am I So Tired?

A FIRST LOOK AT CHILDHOOD DIABETES

PAT THOMAS
ILLUSTRATED BY LESLEY HARKER

BARRON'S

Your body is amazing.
Every day it makes lots
of different substances
that help you think,
play, and stay healthy.

One of these substances is called insulin. It helps your body use the energy that comes from the food you eat.

When you eat, your body turns the food into a special kind of sugar called glucose.

Glucose gives your muscles and your mind the energy to work properly.

Insulin helps keep just the right amount of glucose in your blood. If your body doesn't make enough insulin, you have a condition called diabetes.

Diabetes can make you feel very tired,
shaky, and thirsty.

It can also make you feel like you want
to urinate all the time.

When you feel like this, it's a message from
your body telling you to take care.

11

There are two types of diabetes.

You are born
with the first type.
The second type
you can get at
almost any age.

Your doctor will be able to tell you what type
of diabetes you have. The doctor can also tell
you what to do to help yourself feel better.

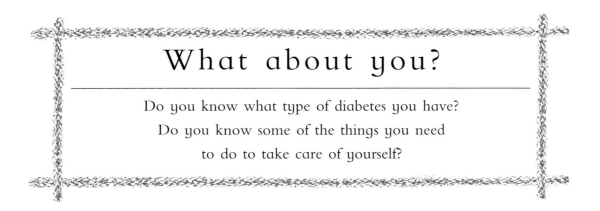

What about you?

Do you know what type of diabetes you have?
Do you know some of the things you need
to do to take care of yourself?

Some children with diabetes need to take medicine every day. They might need to take a pill, have an injection, or wear a special pump that gives them insulin.

To help decide what sort of medicine
you may need when you have diabetes,
you have to check how much
sugar is in your blood every day.

Your parents will do these things for you
for a while. One day, however, you will
be able to do them for yourself.

You may wonder
if one day you
will grow out of
your diabetes.

This won't happen.
Whatever type of
diabetes you have
will stay with you
for life.

But there are lots
of things that you
can do to help
yourself feel better
and stay healthy.

The most important thing you can do
is eat healthy food.

This can be hard when everyone around you
is snacking on sweets and other treats.

But soon you'll learn that eating well means you feel better and have more energy to play with your friends.

What about you?

What sorts of foods do you like eating? Are there some things you used to eat that you can't eat anymore? What are some healthy foods that you know about?

When you have diabetes
it is important to
exercise often.

But remember that exercise uses lots of energy.

You can stop yourself from getting too tired by having a snack before you exercise. Remember to rest if you feel tired.

Sometimes having diabetes can make you feel very different from other children.

You may think you are the only one in the world who has to take medicine or check your blood.

But there are probably other children in your
school or neighborhood who also have it.

Sometimes having diabetes can be hard.
There's so much to remember.

You can't make diabetes go away,
but you can talk about it with your friends,
your family, and your teachers. That way
everybody can understand how you feel and
help you when you need it.

Diabetes means you have
to learn to take care
of yourself in a
special way.

Once you learn to do that, you'll find you can do all the same things other children do and have just as much fun.

HOW TO USE THIS BOOK

A child with diabetes is a child first, and a person with diabetes second. It is unrealistic to expect very young children to fully understand their condition or to take responsibility for it. Use simple language to explain the condition. Make conversation about it (such as about how they feel or what they eat) part of daily life.

During early childhood, parents must take responsibility for all aspects of their diabetic child's care. Experts believe that expecting too much too soon from young children when learning to monitor glucose and control diabetes can lead to low self-esteem. This, in turn, can lead to more mistakes in their self-care and poorer blood-glucose control later.

However, children can be involved in some aspects of their care from an early age. They can, for instance, be offered simple choices, such as which finger to take blood from or where on their body they would prefer to receive an insulin injection.

The more regular you make your child's routine of testing and injections, the easier it will be for him or her to accept it. It is also a good idea to teach your child to recognize low blood sugar and what to do about it.

Be careful of the language you use with your child. Replace the word "test" with "check" or "reading"; and when talking about blood sugar levels, it is better to use the terms "high," "low," and "normal" rather than "good" or "bad." Talk in terms of having diabetes rather than labeling your child a diabetic.

It is natural for parents to worry about their child's health. But being over-protective can make your child feel that diabetes has completely taken over his or her life. Early acknowledgment of your child's feelings about diabetes, and how these sometimes conflict with the normal desires of childhood, will maintain self-esteem. This can help as your child grows up. Teens can be very resentful of their diabetes and the way it sets them apart from others. This is the most likely time to find children rebelling against medication and nutritional approaches.

Communication with caregivers and teachers is vital. Parents should ensure that everyone understands the need for regular insulin injections or how to monitor an insulin pump, and that their child needs to eat regularly and take care before exercise. They should be aware of any activities that might affect the condition, such as sports days. Schools should respect parents' wishes to keep their child's health problems confidential.

School-age children can be given lessons about what medicines (such as insulin) are, what the pancreas does, and how the body converts carbohydrates in food into glucose and uses this for energy. Group discussion can help other children be more aware of the symptoms of low blood sugar and how to help their friends with diabetes. School is an important place to dispel myths and worries such as whether diabetes can be caught from someone else or that people with diabetes can't play sports. As more and more young children are being diagnosed with Type-2 diabetes (which can be caused by poor diet), healthy eating education has an important early role to play in prevention.

BOOKS TO READ

Even Superheroes Get Diabetes
Sue Ganz-Schmitt and Micah Chambers-Goldberg
(Dog Ear Publishing, 2007)

How I Feel: A Book About Diabetes
Michael Olson and Steven Olson
(Lantern Books, 2003)

Rufus Comes Home
Kim Gosselin and Terry Ravanelli
(Jayjo Books, 1998)

Even Little Kids Get Diabetes
Connie White Pirner and Nadine Bernard
Westcott (Albert Whitman & Company, 1994)

Life with Diabetes: Lacie the Lizard's Adventure
Dana Sheppard and Troy Jones
(Critters, Inc., 2004)

RESOURCES FOR ADULTS

American Diabetes Association
ATTN: National Call Center
1701 North Beauregard Street
Alexandria, VA 22311
1-800-DIABETES (1-800-342-2383)
Web: www.diabetes.org

Children with Diabetes
The online community for kids, families, and adults
with diabetes
Web: www.childrenwithdiabetes.com

Juvenile Diabetes Research Foundation
120 Wall Street
New York, NY 10005-4001
Phone: 1-800-533-CURE (2873)
Fax: (212) 785-9595
Web: www.jdrf.org

Books

Your Child Has Diabetes: A Guide for Managing Diabetes in Children. Pritchett & Hull Associates, Inc.
(1-800-241-4925)

The Ten Keys to Helping Your Child with Diabetes. American Diabetes Association (may be ordered on
their Web site)

The Calorie King: Calorie, Fat and Carbohydrate Counter (www.calorieking.com, or at most bookstores)